T0016620

LOOK

I'm an Ecologist

DK

For the grown-ups

This book is full of hands-on activities that will tap right into your child's natural curiosity. Each activity is designed to let your child play and learn with all their senses. Together, you can grow their love of nature and science, as well as their understanding of the world.

Here are a few tips to help you along the way:

Your child should be supervised at all times when doing activities and experiments, but try to give them time and space to lead the direction of play. The questions in this book are suggestions. Let your child ask, and answer, their own questions.

•

Involve your child in each step of the projects. Let them measure, mix, and follow the instructions. Encourage your child to figure things out, and allow them to modify the activity if they would like to.

•

Adult Alert stars show where your child will need extra grown-up help. Before you start an activity, consider any hazards, together, and ways to avoid them. If your child has long hair, make sure it is tied back and out of the way.

Adult ALERT!

•

Protect the area where your child will be playing and encourage them to wear old clothes or an apron. Being prepared lets your child enjoy themselves in the best way they can. Making a mess is part of the fun and learning!

DK Penguin Random House

Written by Cathriona Hickey
Editors Sarah MacLeod, Sophie Parkes
Senior Editor Dawn Sirett
US Editor Jane Perlmutter
Design and Illustration Rachael Hare
Additional Design Karen Hood
Educational Consultant Penny Coltman
Photographer Lol Johnson
Jacket Designer Rachael Hare
Jacket Coordinator Issy Walsh
Production Editor Abi Maxwell
Production Controller Isabell Schart
Managing Editor Penny Smith
Deputy Art Director Mabel Chan
Publishing Director Sarah Larter

First American Edition, 2021
Published in the United States by DK Publishing
1450 Broadway, Suite 801, New York, NY 10018

Copyright © 2021 Dorling Kindersley Limited
DK, a Division of Penguin Random House LLC
21 22 23 24 25 10 9 8 7 6 5 4 3 2 1
001-322923-Sep/2021

A catalog record for this book
is available from the Library of Congress.
ISBN 978-0-7440-3381-6

DK books are available at special discounts when purchased in bulk for sales promotions, premiums, fund-raising, or educational use.
For details, contact: DK Publishing Special Markets,
1450 Broadway, Suite 801, New York, NY 10018
SpecialSales@dk.com

Printed and bound in China

www.dk.com

Picture credits
The publisher would like to thank the following for their kind permission to reproduce their photographs:
(Key: a-above; b-below/bottom; c-centre; f-far; l-left; r-right; t-top)

6 123RF.com: stillfx (cra). 10 Dorling Kindersley: Neil Fletcher (br). Dreamstime.com: Vvoevale (c). 11 Dreamstime.com: Ksushsh (tc, cra); Vvoevale (ca). 12 Dreamstime.com: Anton Starikov (ca). 14 123RF.com: Ruslan Nassyrov (cla). 15 123RF.com: Ruslan Nassyrov (b). 16 123RF.com: Ruslan Nassyrov (cra). 17 Dreamstime.com: Stig Karlsson / Stigsfoto (cb). 20-21 Dreamstime.com: Daboost. 21 Alamy Stock Photo: Andrew Paterson (clb). Dreamstime.com: Toneimage (c). 22 Dreamstime.com: Veronika Oliinyk (cla, cra). 22-23 Dreamstime.com: Isselee (bc). 23 Alamy Stock Photo: blickwinkel / H. Schulz (bc); Sean Campbell (bl); blickwinkel / Schulz (fbr). Dreamstime.com: Isselee (br); Veronika Oliinyk (tr, crb). Getty Images / iStock: Kaphoto (bc/Badger). 28 123RF.com: Václav Šebek (br). Dreamstime.com: Victortyakht (bc). 29 123RF.com: Christian Mueringer (cr). Alamy Stock Photo: Tom Uhlman (bl). 31 Alamy Stock Photo: Philip Jones (bc). 32 Dreamstime.com: Elena Kazanskaya (cra). 34 Dreamstime.com: Katerynabibro (cra). 36 Dreamstime.com: Marina Lohrbach (br). 37 Dreamstime.com: Richard J Thompson / Photoaged (cla); Krzysztof Slusarczyk (br). 38 Dreamstime.com: Katerynabibro (c/bean); Phanuwan (cla); Anton Starikov (c). 40 Dreamstime.com: Carolyn Franks (cla); Liudmyla Havryliuk (c); Penchan Pumila (cr). 41 Dreamstime.com: Carolyn Franks (ca); David Moreno (tc); Tatiana Neelova (bl); Wirestock (bc). 45 123RF.com: (cl); Martin Spurny (c). Dreamstime.com: Photka (c/Trash, bc); Svitlana Ponurkina (tl); Roberto Giovannini / HP_Proprietario (crb)

Cover images: Front: Dreamstime.com: Michael Truchon clb

All other images © Dorling Kindersley
For further information see: www.dkimages.com

MIX
Paper from responsible sources
FSC™ C018179

Contents

Little minds have big ideas!

Ecologists study **plants**, **animals**, and the places where they live, called **environments**. You can be an ecologist too! You just need to ask **questions**, and use **your brain** and **your senses** to answer them!

Curious questions

Start thinking like an ecologist! Here are some questions to ask yourself as you play.

- When I see or hear an animal, what is it doing? Is it calling to other animals? Is it looking for food? Is it building a nest? Is it hiding to keep itself safe?

- When I look at a plant, what can I see? Are new shoots growing? Have animals been eating it? Does it look like it needs water? Do the flowers on it smell nice? How might that help the plant?

- Are there things I can do to help plants and animals?

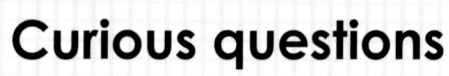

Your ecologist senses

Brain

Your brain is not one of your senses, but it gathers information from them all and helps you understand it.

Hearing

Animals make lots of noises. Listen carefully when you are outside. What can you hear?

Sight

Awesome ecologists use their eyes to spot animal clues, such as paw prints, spider's webs, or frog eggs.

Smell

Nature is full of interesting smells. Use your nose to smell flowers, soil, or wet leaves.

Taste

Your tongue is great at tasting different food flavors. Try growing some herbs to add to your food.

Touch

Your skin tells you how things feel. Be careful with plants that might be prickly and animals that might sting.

Let's go explore the world around us!

Nature treasures

A **nature walk** is a great way to **see** nature. Collect **treasures** such as leaves, fallen flowers, and feathers. Use them in these crafts to **remember** what you found.

You will need:

bucket for collecting treasures

safety scissors

hole punch

heavy book

PVA glue

card stock

string, ribbon, or yarn

duct tape

stick

Flower and leaf bookmark

Create a **bookmark** using the **flowers** and **leaves** you find on your walk.

1 Carefully lay the **flowers** and **leaves** between two pieces of **card stock**. Then put the card stock in between the pages of a **heavy book** and close it.

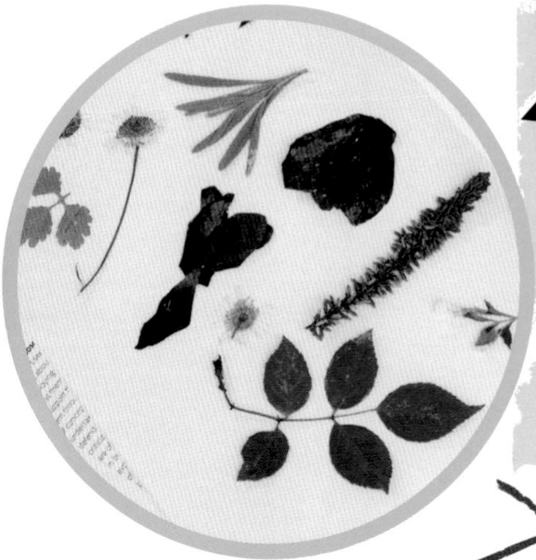

2

After a few days, take the **flowers** and **leaves** out of the book. Be very careful—they will be **fragile**!

Adult ALERT!

3

Use **safety scissors** to **cut** a piece of **card stock** about 2 in (5 cm) wide by 20 cm (8 in) long.

Use a hole punch to make a hole in the top of the card stock and tie a piece of string, ribbon, or yarn through the hole.

4

Make a **beautiful design** with the pressed flowers and leaves on the card stock, then **glue** them in place.

Nature memory stick

A **memory stick** is perfect for keeping a **collection** of things you find on your nature walk.

1 Put dots of **glue** along the stick where you want to place your nature treasures. Then gently **press** the treasures onto the glue.

2 Tie **string, ribbon, or yarn** to the stick for extra decoration. You can plant your stick in a **flowerpot**, and display it in your room.

Collect treasures that have different colors and textures.

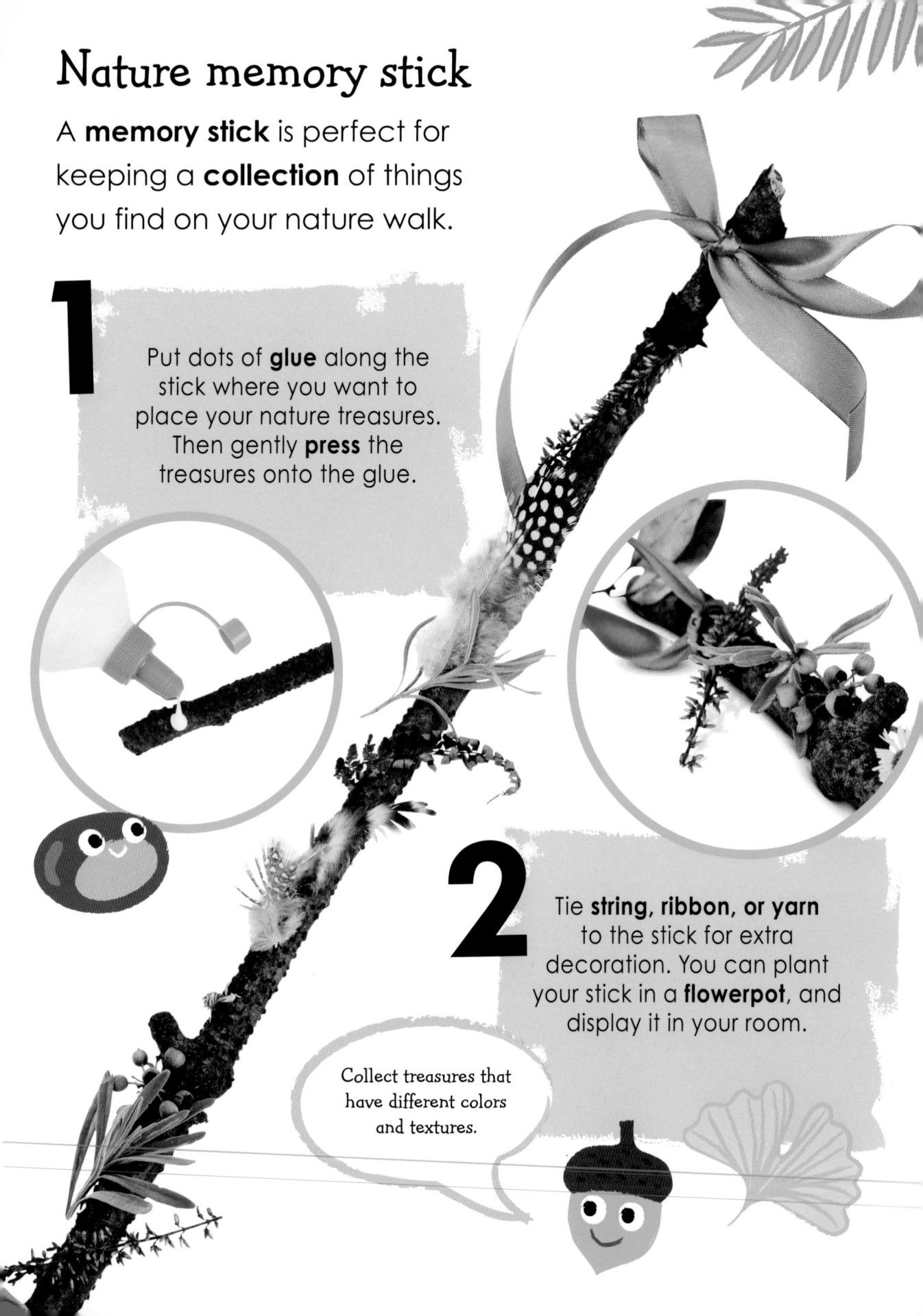

Beautiful bracelet

This **sticky bracelet** is a great way to **collect** nature treasures as you go!

1 Ask an adult to wrap a piece of **duct tape** around your wrist with the **sticky side out**, and attach the ends to make a loop.

Adult ALERT!

2 Go on a nature walk to **collect** fallen leaves, flowers, feathers, and twigs. **Press** each treasure you find onto your sticky bracelet.

By the end of your adventure, you will have a bracelet full of the beautiful things you found along the way.

Wonderful trees!

There are so many **types of trees** in the world.
Let's use **art** to see how they are **different**!

You will need:

paint

paintbrushes

PVA glue

crayons

paper

fallen leaves

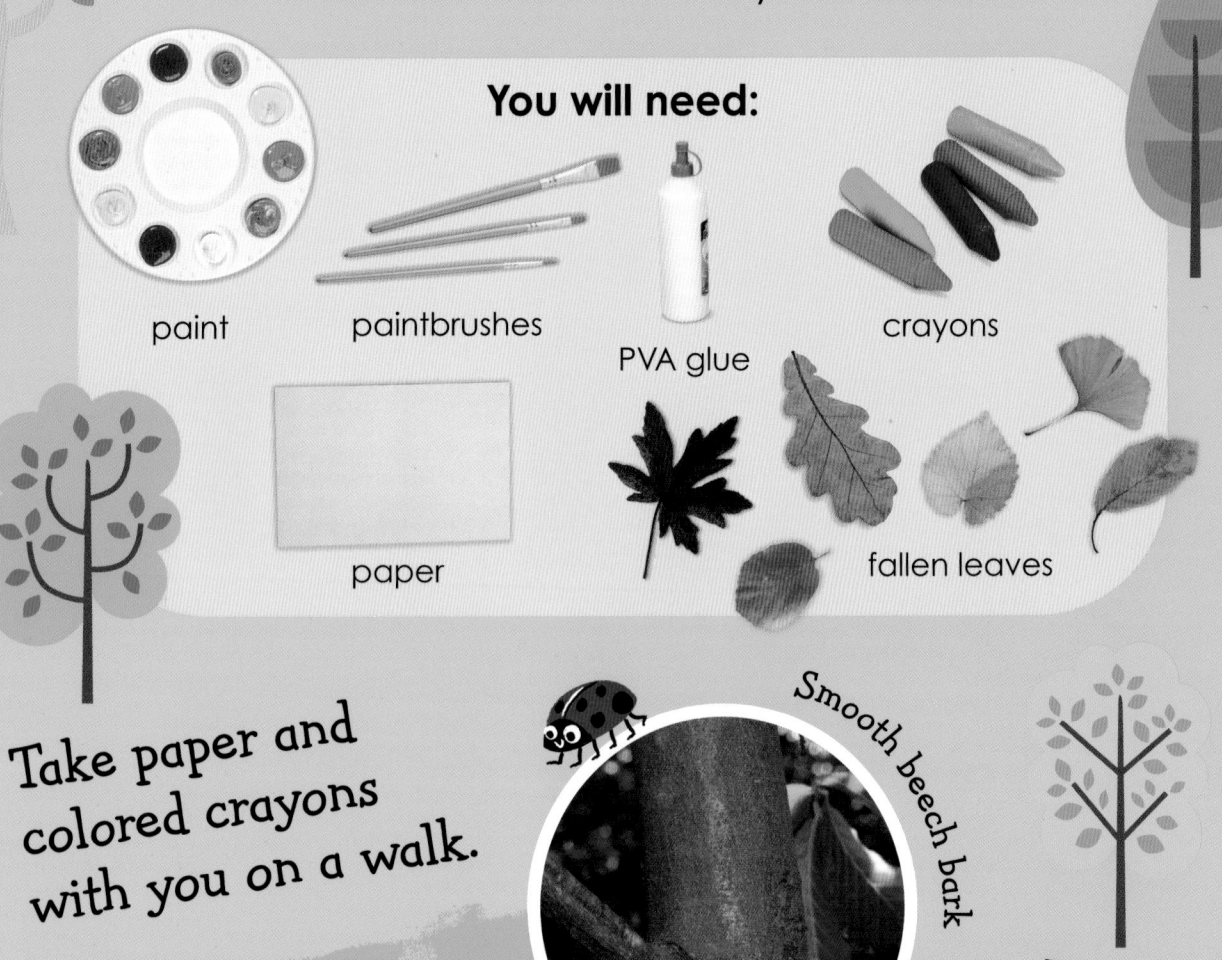

Take paper and colored crayons with you on a walk.

Smooth beech bark

Bumpy willow bark

Bark clues

Lean your paper against the **bark** of a tree. **Rub** the side of your **crayon** on the paper. What happens? Try another tree—does it look different?

1
Leaf clues

Collect fallen leaves that are different **colors, shapes, and sizes.** Let the leaves dry at home, if they are wet.

The leaves of each type of tree look different.

2

Paint the leaves in your favorite colors, then let them dry. **Arrange** your leaves on a piece of **paper** and stick them down with glue.

What shapes are your leaves?

Long and wide with wavy edges

Long and thin with smooth edges

Start a nature gallery to display your tree art!

Who is it?

How many different **bugs** can you **name**?
Collect bugs from in your **yard** or at the **park**,
and see if you can name them all.

You will need:

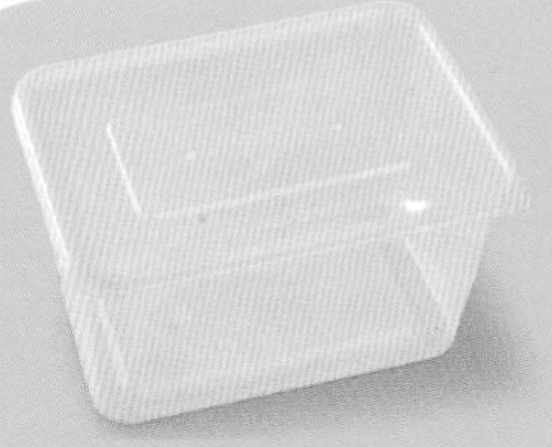

shallow plastic
container

soil

magnifying glass

paper

leaves and moss

small pebbles

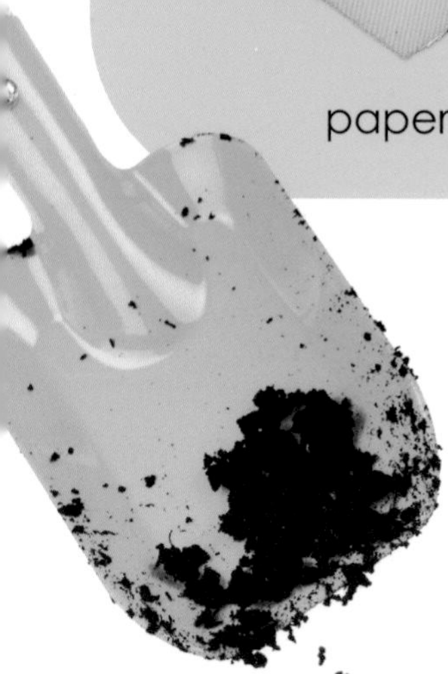

1

Put a thin layer of
soil in the plastic
container. Add
pebbles, leaves,
and **moss**.

2

In your yard or at the park, **look** for a bug under dead wood, rocks, or leaves. **Lay** the paper next to the bug and **wait** for it to crawl onto the paper.

ADULT ALERT!

You MUST put the animal back safely where you found it as soon as you've looked at it.

3

Once it is on the paper, **carefully** place the bug in your container.

EXPLORE ecology

How many legs does the bug have?

Let it crawl on your hand. How does it feel?

How many body parts can you name?

Look closely at the animal with a magnifying glass.

A snack for the birds

In winter it can be tricky for **birds** to find **food. Help** the birds when they need it most by making these two tempting **bird feeders.**

For the pine-cone feeder, you will need:

pine cone

peanut butter

seeds

string and safety scissors

shallow container

wood knife

1

Pine-cone feeder

Wrap a piece of **string** around the wider end of the pine cone and **tie a knot.**

Use about 24 in (60 cm) of string.

2

Use the wood knife to **coat** the pine cone with a thick layer of **peanut butter**.

Hang your finished feeder from a branch outside, then stand back and watch the birds that come to use it.

How many different types of birds use your feeder? Are they big or small? What colors are they?

3

Pour your seeds into the container and **roll** your pine cone in the seeds. **Hang** the feeder outside.

Make sure your feeder is tied on well!

If you don't have peanut butter

or a pine cone, keep the birds well fed with this bottle feeder.

For the bottle feeder, you will need:

two sticks (these need to be at least twice the width of the bottle)

shallow container

string and scissors

small plastic bottle

seeds

Adult ALERT

1

Bottle feeder

Ask an adult to carefully **cut** two pairs of holes in the bottle. Each pair should be opposite each other. **Push** the sticks through the holes.

2

Above each stick, cut a feeding hole about 0.4 in (1 cm) wide. **Fill** the bottle with **seeds** and screw the lid on.

Try using a mix of different seeds.

Try using different types of seeds or nuts in your feeder. Do some birds prefer one thing over another?

Woodpeckers love peanuts

Tie a long piece of string around the bottle and hang it outside for birds to perch on.

17

Bug home

Bugs like a **home** that provides them with **food**, **shelter**, and **water**. This **bug habitat** provides a place for different animals to live together.

You will need:

small twigs (or bamboo sticks if you have them)

about ten long twigs

string

pebbles

leaves

pine cones

cardboard

safety scissors

crayons

1

Find a patch of soil outside. Arrange the **long twigs** in a cone shape. **Tie string** around the top to hold the sticks together.

2

Lay the **pebbles** inside your habitat, then layer small **twigs** or **bamboo sticks, pine cones**, and **leaves** on top.

Shhh! After a few days, peek inside to see who has moved in!

Cut out a triangle of cardboard for a door.

What's the **weather** like?

Recording the **weather** and learning how **animals** and **plants** deal with different conditions is an important part of being an ecologist.

You will need a notebook with seven pages, or a large piece of paper.

Label each page with each day of the week and the date, like this:

Adult ALERT

Ask an adult for help if you need help with writin

Monday

DATE _____

. . . .

. . . .

. . . .

. . . .

. . . .

Do you see sun? Do you feel rain or snow? Do you hear wind?

Look outside. What is the weather like? What do you **see**, **feel**, and **hear**?

Watch the weather for seven days. Does it **change**?

Draw or **write** about the weather in your notebook.

How do you get **ready** for the weather? Do you wear **boots** if it rains? Do you wear a **hat** if it's sunny?

How do animals protect themselves in different types of weather?

Can you see any animals enjoying the weather?

Draw a picture of an **animal** that likes the rain and one that likes the sun.

Mud prints

Animals and ecologists **love** mud!
Animals like to **roll in it** and ecologists like to
look in it to **learn all about them.**

You will need:

plastic animals

mixing bowl

cocoa powder

water

flour

Mix everything together to make a **thick** mud.

Put the **ingredients** in your **bowl.**

Let the mixture dry a little.

Walk your plastic animals through the **mud**. Think about what they would do in the wild— birds **hop**, horses **trot**, and goats **charge**!

Next time you are on a nature walk, look for tracks in the mud. Can you spot the tracks of a deer, raccoon, badger, or fox? What do your tracks look like?

Hide your animals and ask someone to **guess** which animal made each **track**. Give them clues—heavier animals leave deeper prints.

Deer prints

Badger prints

Fox prints

23

Spider weave

Spiders build **webs** to **catch** bugs to eat. Can you **weave** a string web to **trap** a tasty treat?

You will need:

string   safety scissors   sticks

1 Lay your sticks so they **cross over** each other to make a **star shape**.

The bigger the sticks, the bigger the web!

2 **Wrap** and **tie** pieces of **string** around the sticks where they meet in the **middle**. Do this across each of the **diagonals**.

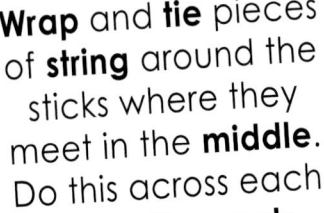

3

Tie a **very long** piece of **string** to a stick near the center of the star. Then **wrap** the string around the next stick.

Hang your web from a tree in the yard or doorway in your house.

4

Continue, **twisting** the string around each stick until you reach the **edge** of the star. When you reach the end, tie a **knot**.

Did you know spiders are arachnids, not insects? Arachnids have eight legs, while insects have just six.

Nest building

Chicks need a **safe** and **sturdy** place to **hatch** and be **fed** by their parents. Let's see if you can build a **strong nest** of your own!

You will need:

paper plate

safety scissors

hole punch

air dry clay

nest materials

small sticks

1

Make **holes** around the **edge** of the plate. The holes should be about a **finger width** apart.

EXPLORE ecology

Does your nest feel safe and strong?

How deep does it need to be to keep the eggs safe?

What happens to the nest when it rains? Test it outside!

2 **Weave** sticks through the holes to create a **sturdy frame**.

Add leaves, moss, and feathers to make it soft and cozy.

Make pretend eggs from air dry clay, and put them in your nest like real eggs! Birds lay eggs in a nest and take care of the chicks there when they hatch.

27

Sounds of nature

Can you make your **very own orchestra** from nature?
Head out on a **nature walk** to collect natural
bits and pieces to **use as instruments**.

Collect what you find in a bucket.

Animal sounds

Nature makes a lot of **noise**!
Wild animals will **make
a racket** for all sorts
of reasons.

Birds **sing** to **warn** other birds of danger.

Badgers **growl** when they **play**.

With your instruments:

Knock two together— do they make a sound?

Shake some of the things you find in a can—what sounds do they make?

Can you make up a song about your walk and play along with your instruments?

Lots of things in nature can be instruments!

acorns

shake together

knock against a tree

chestnuts

pine cones

rub together

twigs

tap

leaves

stones

rustle

roll along the ground

seeds

rattle

Foxes **scream** to get the **attention** of other foxes.

Frog life cycle stone story

Paint your own froggy **life cycle** to see what it takes for **frog eggs** to grow into adult **frogs**.

You will need:

5 large stones, washed and dried

marker

paint

Each stone will show a different stage of a frog's life cycle.

paintbrush

paper

Paint

the five different stages of a frog's life that you see here.

frog eggs

What other life cycles can you paint?

tadpole

adult frog

Lay your stones in a **circle** on a piece of paper. Draw **arrows** between each stone to show which way the **cycle** goes.

froglet

tadpole with legs

Next time you pass a pond, look closely to see if you can spot any of the frog stages!

Frogs are **amphibians**. They can live both in **water** and on **land**. Changing from one form to another, like from a tadpole to a froglet, is called **metamorphosis**. The frog looks completely **different** at each stage!

31

Make your own soil!

Soil provides **energy** for **plants** to grow big and strong. You can make your own soil, called **compost**, using **leftover food**.

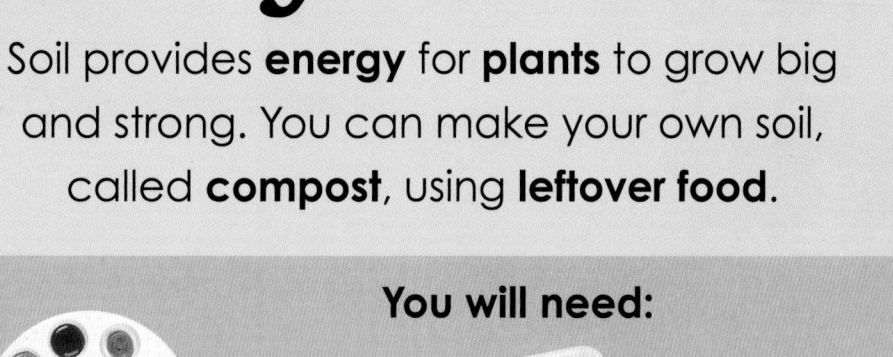

You will need:

paint

plastic container with lid

pen

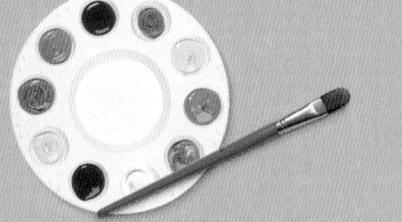

used coffee grounds

dead leaves

egg shells

fruit and vegetable scraps

shredded newspaper

cardboard

ADULT ALERT!

Use the **pen** to make **holes** in the **lid**. These will let **air** get to the compost.

Decorate your container

EXPLORE ecology

What's that smell? All the food and leaves in your compost are slowly breaking down. It can get pretty smelly!

Does the compost feel warm? This is because tiny organisms are working hard to break it down. In cold weather you might even see steam coming from it! Wash your hands after touching the compost.

Fill your box with the scraps, leaves, newspaper, egg shells, and cardboard, then put it **outside**. In a few months it will **break down** to form **nutrient-rich compost!**

Compost provides food to lots of living things, such as worms, bacteria (tiny organisms), and fungi.

Will it grow?

What do **plants** need to **grow**?
Let's grow some **beans** to find out.

What you will need:

3 tall glasses
(clear glass is best
so you can see the
bean sprout)

cotton balls

water

3 beans
(any bean seeds will
work, such as pinto
or fava beans)

1

Label your glasses
A, B, and C, and fill
each one two-thirds
full with **cotton balls**.
Place a **bean** in each
glass on top of the
cotton balls.

2

Sprinkle glasses
A and B with
water to **wet** the
cotton balls. Let the
cotton balls
in glass C **dry**.

3 **Leave** each **glass** in the following places for **two weeks**:

Window sill

A

Dark box or cupboard

B

Window sill

C

4 **Check** on your beans **every few days**. Add more water to A and B if they look dry. Which bean grows **tallest**?

If you don't have any cotton balls, paper towels will work too!

A This bean has **water, light**, and **air** so it should grow the best.

B This bean should sprout, but it won't grow because it has **no light**.

C This bean should not sprout or grow because it has **no water**.

35

Flowers for bees and butterflies

Bees and **butterflies** love to drink a delicious liquid called **nectar** that's found inside **flowers**. By growing flowers, you can help these **important insects**.

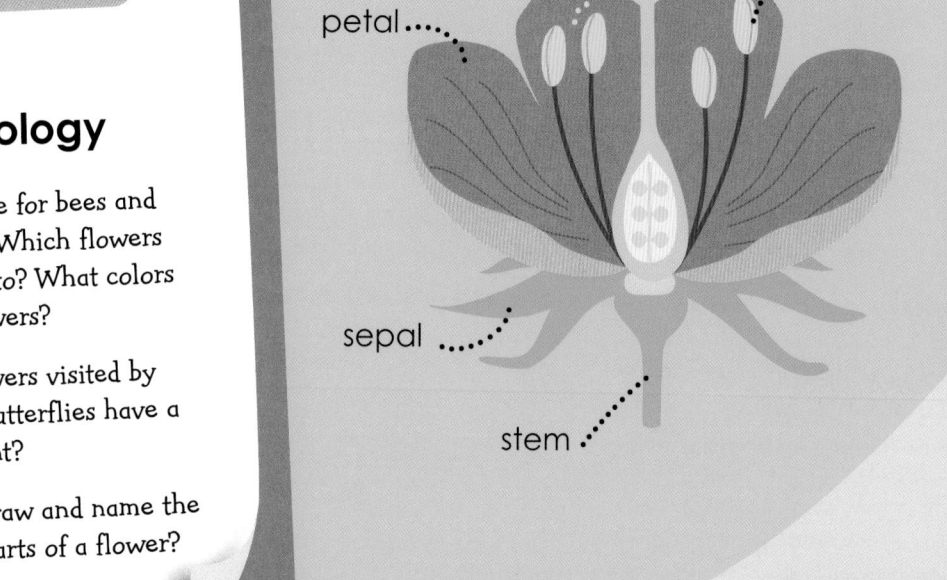

pollen

stamen

petal

sepal

stem

echinacea

EXPLORE ecology

 Look outside for bees and butterflies. Which flowers do they go to? What colors are the flowers?

 Do the flowers visited by bees and butterflies have a strong scent?

 Can you draw and name the different parts of a flower?

Here are some ideas for flowers you can grow that bees and butterflies love.

When you help bees and butterflies, you help plants, too! Without them, many plants wouldn't grow.

Pollination

As the insects fly from **flower to flower**, the **pollen** on them is rubbed off onto parts of other flowers. This is called **pollination**. It helps plants make **seeds** so new plants can grow.

Feeding time

Butterflies and bees use their **long tongues** to drink **nectar** from flowers. As they drink, they rub against a **powder** on the flowers' stamens, called **pollen**, which **sticks** to their bodies.

sunflower

lavender

hemp agrimony

calendula

Paper plant pots

Growing plants is great fun, but to get started you need **pots**. Let's find out how to **make your own**.

You will need:

paper-towel rolls cut in half

plastic container

newspaper or magazine

safety scissors

soil

seeds

glass

Cardboard pots

Fold each flap over to cover the opening.

Cut four 1 in (2.5 cm) slits in one end of an empty half **paper-towel roll** to create four **flaps. Repeat** with the other rolls.

Stand your **cardboard pots** in a **plastic container**. Fill them with **soil**, then they're ready for you to start **planting seeds**!

Newspaper pots

Take a sheet of **newspaper** and **fold** it twice lengthwise.

Wrap the folded newspaper around a glass or bottle.

Fold the newspaper over the **base** of the glass, then remove the glass to leave your **newspaper pot**.

Try growing food in your pots. That means the food travels less to get to you, which is better for the planet.

Homegrown

Homegrown food is not only **good for the planet,** but **tastes delicious**, too—**let's get growing!**

You will need:

3 plant pots

compost

water

tomato seeds

red pepper seeds

basil seeds

1

Fill each pot three-quarters full with **compost.**

Compost is **packed** full of **nutrients.**

2

Push your **finger** into the compost to make a small **hole**.

When is your food is ready to pick?

Tomatoes and peppers should be plump and red and come off the stalk easily.

Basil leaves should be long and green.

3

Put the tomato **seeds** into a hole, then **cover** with a little compost. Do the same with the pepper and basil seeds in the other two pots.

4

Water the seeds, then put your pots on a **sunny** window sill.

Make sure you keep your compost moist. Check it every morning and add some water if it feels dry.

Try the food you have grown. What's your favorite?

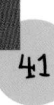

Terrific tide pool

Tide pools are found on **rocky shores**. They form when **water gets trapped** on and between rocks as the **tide goes out**.

You will need:

large bowl
or bucket

sand

water

modelng tools

air dry clay

rocks and pebbles

shells (optional)

You can make your own tide pool. First you need to make some animals to live there.

Form little **sea creatures** out of your air dry clay, such as **crabs** and **starfish**.

Let's build your tide pool

1

Spread a layer of **sand** in the **bowl**.

2

Place **rocks**, **pebbles** and **shells** around the edge of the sand. Pour some **water** in.

3

Now your animals are ready to **dive into** their **habitat**!

...you can add some **seaweed**!

If you live near the **seaside**...

Sea creatures live in tide pools, making a home until the tide comes back in. An animal's home is called a habitat.

43

I can save the planet!

Our planet needs our **help!** Here are some ways we can all **protect the planet**.

Plastic in the oceans can harm sea creatures.

Try to buy food wrapped in paper so there's less plastic waste at home.

1

Use the same **shopping bags** more than once.

2

Make sure your **water bottle** is one you can **reuse** again and again!

3

Look for the **recyclable** symbol on things you buy. Then help **separate** the **recycling** from the trash at home.

4

Try not to **waste food** or materials. You can put food waste in a **compost bin**.

5

Do your own **upcycling**! Use **old** items to make **new** ones.

WOW!

Look, you're an ecologist!

Awesome ecologists (like you) use their **brains**, their **creativity**, and all their **senses** to explore the **amazing world** around them, and to make it a little **happier**.

Why do things happen?

Ecologists use their senses to understand what is happening in nature. It's all about watching and learning from the world around us.

How do we protect nature?

Ecologists work hard to protect nature. From designing a home for bugs to making a feeder for birds, there are endless ways for you to protect nature too.

Is that new?

Ecologists spend their time out and about in nature, so they discover new plants, fungi, and animals all the time! Be sure to keep your eyes open—you never know what you might find.

Don't give up!

It's okay if something you create to help nature doesn't work on the first try. Keep watching the world around you and trying new approaches until you find one that works.

Try to think of other ways to help the plants and animals in the area around your home.

Well done! You're an ecologist!

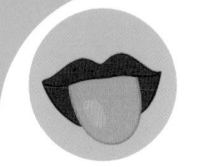
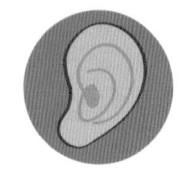
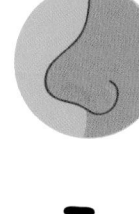
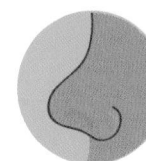

Index

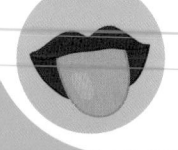
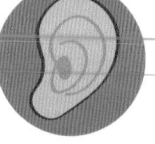
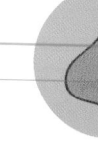
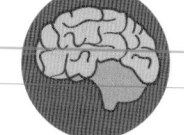
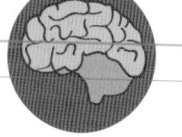
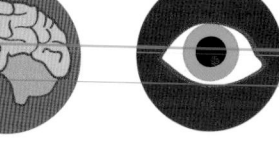
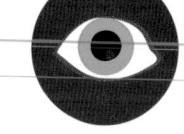